wedding
FLOWERS

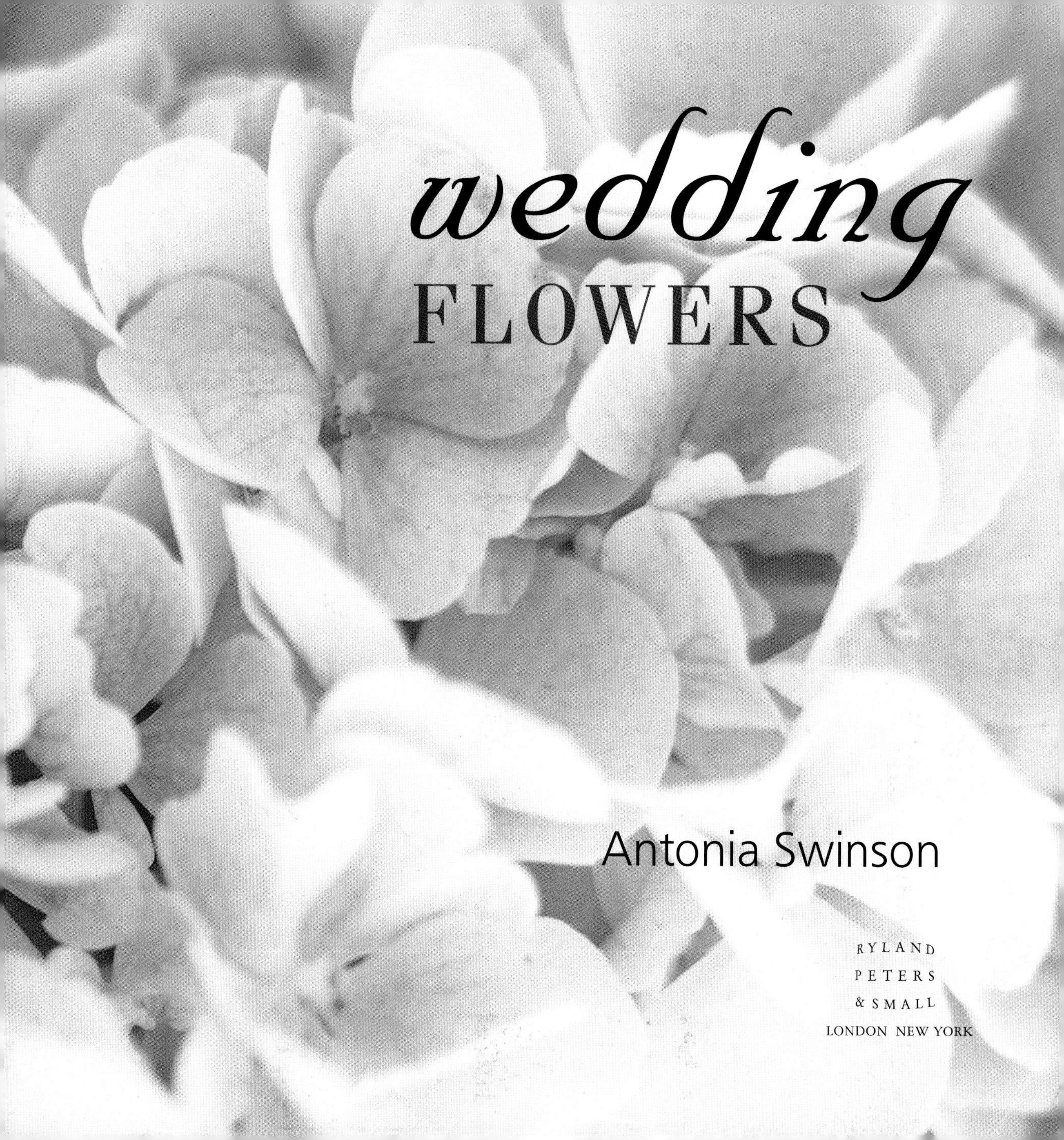

wedding FLOWERS

Antonia Swinson

RYLAND
PETERS
& SMALL
LONDON NEW YORK

Senior Designer	Liz Sephton
Senior Editor	Clare Double
Picture Research	Emily Westlake
Production	Gemma Moules
Publishing Director	Alison Starling

First published in the UK in 2008 by
Ryland Peters & Small
20–21 Jockey's Fields
London WC1R 4BW
www.rylandpeters.com

10 9 8 7 6 5 4 3 2 1

Text, design and photographs
© Ryland Peters & Small 2008

ISBN: 978-1-84597-455-8
A catalogue record for this book is
available from the British Library.

Printed and bound in China.

contents

Introduction

Every wedding is a reflection of the personalities and
tastes of the bride and groom. Flowers play a big part in
setting the scene for the day and, depending on which
varieties are chosen, their colours and the designs they are
part of, can help to conjure up any number of different
styles and moods. Nowadays there isn't a high street in
the land on which you can't buy a huge range of flowers
sourced from all over the world. This breadth of choice
opens up all kinds of possibilities but it can be hard to
know where to start, particularly if you are unfamiliar
with flowers and how they're arranged.

    This book is designed to inspire and inform, to act
as a comprehensive style resource for anyone embarking

on the process of choosing their wedding flowers. There are sections covering all the sorts of arrangements you might want on the day: bridal bouquets; flowers for the bridesmaids; floral headdresses and accessories; buttonholes and corsages; and flowers for the reception, including table centrepieces, place settings and favours. Each section covers lots of different styles of arrangement and uses of colour. There are colour schemes which are pale, vibrant, cool and hot; and styles such as traditional, modern, romantic, minimalist, formal and rustic.

The first decision to be taken about flowers is usually what the bride will carry, and from this key starting point ideas can develop for all the other floral arrangements needed on the day. Sometimes a bride will have particular flowers in mind for her bouquet, such as roses or lilies. Sometimes colour will be the key: the bride might want all her wedding flowers to be white or cream, for instance.

The style which the bride and groom are aspiring to is crucial: for example, if the wedding is to be modern and minimalist, certain flowers will reflect this better than others (calla lilies and orchids have the right sort of structural quality; carnations don't). Or, if the wedding is a laid-back family occasion at the local village church, with the reception in a marquee, cottage-garden flowers such as sweet peas, pinks and stocks will be a charming

complement. The seasons can play an influential role, too. For a wedding taking place just before Christmas, for instance, what could be more natural than to be inspired by the colours of the season: the dark green of evergreen foliage; the red of holly berries and the white of snow and frost? In spring, the presence of lots of white, yellow and blue flowers in the landscape might inspire a palette of narcissi, spring snowflakes and forget-me-nots.

Choosing your wedding flowers should be a happy and exciting process, and whether your taste runs to a big bouquet of electric-blue dyed roses or a little posy of lily of the valley picked from the garden, flowers will help to make your day the glorious celebration you've dreamed of.

Flowers for the Bride

Introduction

The bride is undeniably the star of any wedding, so
her flowers are also the focus of much attention. The
wedding dress is the key stylistic element of the day,
so its design, fabric and colour will shape ideas for the
bouquet. A traditional white or off-white dress is a
flattering backdrop to flowers of any colour, from whites
and pastels to brights. If the dress is a different colour,
whether palest pink or rich gold, the flowers need to be
chosen with more care to avoid an unflattering clash.

White is still the classic choice for the bouquet as
much as the dress; pastels are romantic and easy to work
with; deeper colours, such as rich purples or sultry reds,
are trickier to use but can look spectacular. Certain
colours seem to lend themselves to the quality of the light

in each season: blue-reds and greens in winter; blue, white and yellow in spring; clear, bright pinks, blues and purples in the strong summer light; and warm, mellow yellows and oranges in autumn. Think about the shape of the bouquet, too. The most traditional is a teardrop or 'shower' shape, using wired flowers, though simpler tied bouquets are now very popular. You could also opt for a generous bouquet designed to be carried over the arm.

Whether you choose a large, loose bouquet or a neat, domed one depends partly on the shape of your dress; don't let the flowers dominate the ensemble. For instance, a sheaf of calla lilies would perfectly complement a slim column dress, while a full-skirted gown could carry off a large, dramatic bouquet.

TRADITIONAL
BOUQUETS
cool and pastel colours

The stems of this bouquet are bound in striped ribbon, secured with pearl-headed pins.
The colour scheme is white with tiny touches of *blue and pink*, achieved with roses,
stocks, veronicas, larkspurs and *cornflowers*.

This large, loose bouquet, tied with wide white ribbon, has a *cottage-garden feel*. The round, soft *peonies* complement the roses well, with *delicate dill flowers* and bridal wreath flowers and foliage adding further interest.

This white bouquet is *timelessly elegant*. With its fanned shape, it's designed to be carried gracefully *over the arm*, showing off to the full its combination of roses, loosestrife, lilac and *eucalyptus*, all tied with sheer white ribbon.

Grand but not overly formal, this *dramatic*, hand-tied shower bouquet for a *winter wedding* contrasts pure white flowers with dark, glossy foliage. Exquisite *camellias* and early-flowering clematis partner their own foliage and cascading lengths of ivy.

This tied bouquet, finished with *sheer pink ribbon*, has a nicely compact, full look which shows off the *soft roundness* of the flower heads beautifully. It uses lavender and ruscus foliage, hyacinths, bouvardia, alliums and *snapdragons*.

This bouquet is bigger, looser and more dramatic. It's composed of *huge pink lilies* and roses, *photinia foliage* and flowers, kangaroo paw and *pink-budded jasmine*, all tied with a large bow of bronze-green ribbon.

Although painstakingly made, this wired, teardrop bouquet has a lovely *sense of movement*.
The emphasis is on colour, with *pale and deep pink roses*, lilac and purple Singapore orchids,
veronicas, ruscus foliage and *asparagus fern*.

This dense mass of blooms – three varieties of rose, stock and *freesia* – tied with
old-gold ribbon, is a romantic combination of white, cream and soft pink, with
wired *diamanté beads* adding sparkle.

Traditional Bouquets • Cool and Pastel Colours

This sheaf of calla or arum lilies is spectacular in its *sculptural simplicity*. The long stems have been tied with very wide, *pewter ribbon*, producing an arrangement which would be the ideal match for a *column dress*.

Flowers for the Bride

These *scented longiflorum lilies* have been given a more relaxed treatment by making a few stems into a loose bunch with white *loosestrife*, whose graceful, *arching heads* complement the lilies' tapering petals.

This little bouquet of pink-and-white *ranunculuses* couldn't be simpler or *prettier*.
The stems have been bound with layered satin ribbon, *lace* and velvet ribbon,
fastened with a bead on a pin.

Green and pink is always a pleasing combination and this full bouquet partners
pinky-mauve roses and green-and-pink *hydrangeas*, with the unusual
accompaniment of *poppy seed heads* and marjoram.

Soft pink, lilac and green create a **restful scheme** in this summer bouquet. There are blowsy peonies and roses, **blue flag irises**, clematis, and hebe and skimmia foliage, tied with ribbons in purple and **cerise**.

Flowers for the Bride

The long tails of ribbon tying this bouquet are reminiscent of maypoles and contribute to its *informal, rustic look*. Roses, lupins, *delphiniums*, stocks and marguerites in white, pink, yellow and blue look *fresh and summery*.

True blues are rare in the flower world, but this large, cascading bouquet uses some of the best examples. Stately delphiniums, *sea holly* and ivy erupt from a base of sky-blue *mophead hydrangeas*.

In the garden, lilac is a *herald of early summer*. For this large bouquet, two varieties have
been casually bunched together, their long stems bound with wide, *deep purple ribbon*
and white lace, then finished with a flamboyant bow.

Traditional Bouquets • Cool and Pastel Colours

Bridal bouquets have their origins in the *posies of herbs* once carried on the wedding day to ward off evil spirits. Traditional *ribbon streamers* decorate this modern version, composed of rosemary, *golden marjoram*, thyme, sage and tarragon.

Flowers for the Bride

This bouquet is in the formal *Victorian style*, with the flowers wired into circles. However, a cool palette of green and blue in the form of galax leaves, *guelder rose*, hyacinths and *lisianthus* gives it a modern slant.

TRADITIONAL
BOUQUETS
hot and intense colours

Sweet peas usually come in a *glorious array* of white, pink, purple and red. These, however, are an exceptional mixture of *cream, yellow, apricot and orange* and have been gathered into a huge bunch with *lady's mantle* for contrast.

In a variation, the same sweet peas have been interspersed with huge, *scarlet anemones* to make a **bold** but not garish bouquet. Egg-yolk yellow ribbon and a *ruff of lemon-yellow* net add to the vivacious effect.

This intensely coloured, *sophisticated bouquet* of roses, senecio, galax and *silvery cones* has been designed for a *winter wedding*, when the thin light will heighten the drama of the blue-toned reds and cool greens.

Another winter bouquet, this time its deep reds and greens *lifted* by the inclusion of *white*.
Four varieties of rose have been joined by *skimmia buds* and leaves, laurustinus and
black-berried ivy.

Red and pink is a ***daring combination*** but the result here is stunning. A mixture of pink, red and ***black-red roses*** has been used, along with sweet peas, scarlet ***glory lilies*** and skimmia, finished with a funky checked ribbon.

This dressy bouquet of *white and purple ranunculuses*, black-red roses and pink and purple sweet peas, its stems bound with *gleaming ribbon*, suggests a late-afternoon wedding and evening reception, black tie and dancing.

The poppy anemones, ranunculuses and sweet peas in this bouquet span the purple spectrum, from *lilac* to plum and *royal purple*, with sumptuous and dramatic results. *Two ribbons*, one satin, one sheer, finish the arrangement.

The shape of this bouquet of glowing poppy anemones, lilac and *hebe foliage* is very different to the one opposite. It is unstructured and *naturalistic*, suggesting, perhaps, a laid-back *country wedding* rather than a grand metropolitan one.

43

CONTEMPORARY
BOUQUETS
cool and pastel colours

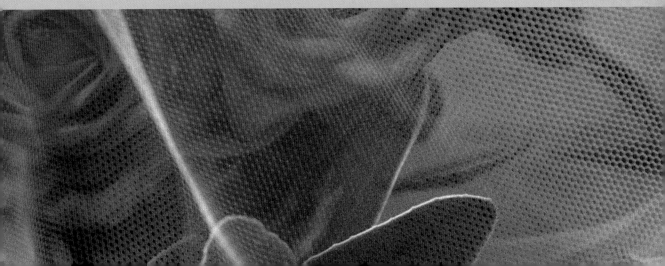

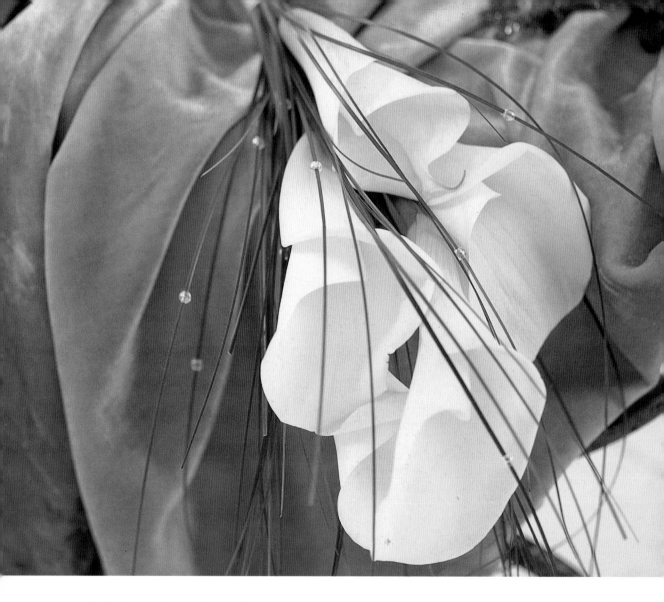

This bouquet of magnificent calla or arum lilies is ***cool and modern***. The stems' length is emphasized by the blades of ***bear grass***, some of which have clear beads threaded onto them. Sheer lilac ribbon and ***silver beaded wire*** (just seen) bind the stems.

This winter bouquet shows that even bare twigs can look glamorous and beautiful. *Willow stems* and skimmia leaves have been *misted with gold* paint spray and arranged with *white roses*, then tied with gold ribbon.

Contemporary Bouquets • Cool and Pastel Colours

Simple and classic, this bouquet of white roses proves the old adage that *less is more*.
A bow of diaphanous ribbon is a good way of echoing an *accent colour* – matching the
bridesmaids' dresses, for example.

Roses which have absorbed dyed water through their stems are available in some extraordinary colours. These *electric blue* ones will only appeal to a few, but *swathed in tulle* and partnered by senecio leaves they look unmistakably *bridal*.

These ranunculuses show how interesting pale can be. With their huge black, *feathery centres* and *pink-tinged white petals*, they're undeniably glamorous, particularly when finished with a collar of *silver organza* and cranberry ribbon.

Eucharis lilies have an **exotic and fragile** beauty. Here, the bride, who wears an understated silk column dress, holds a small, loose posy of them to complement the **luxurious minimalism** of her ensemble.

This dense bouquet of lemon-yellow tulips is warm and cheerful, its stems bound in *cream wire-edged ribbon*. Tulips are *star flowers*, being good value, long lasting and available all year in *myriad colours*.

Neat, light and *easy to carry*, the stems of this bouquet of pompom-like *mimosa* and miniature narcissi are bound by exquisite *floral braid*, a detail which is as much a thing of beauty as the flowers themselves.

With its slender, *grass-green leaves* and lantern-like orange flowers, *sandersonia* is a
beautiful oddity. It's so distinctive that it deserves to be used alone, here gathered into
a huge, loose sheaf and tied with *bronze organza ribbon*.

This **green on green** bouquet mixes exotic cymbidium orchids, **kangaroo paw** and galax leaves with frothy lady's mantle, a **cottage-garden favourite**. It's unconventional, certainly, but shows what scope an all-green colour scheme can offer.

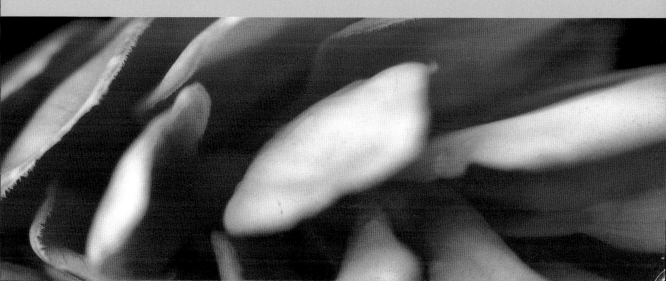

CONTEMPORARY
BOUQUETS
hot and intense colours

Although tulips are spring flowering in the garden, they're available in florists all year. Here, in rich *orange and maroon*, they have an *autumnal* feel. Binding the stems in heavy wire gives the arrangement a *contemporary twist*.

Flowers for the Bride

This grand, even extravagant, bouquet puts the focus on *intense colour*, with roses, *Iceland poppies* and ranunculuses in shades of *burnt orange*, tangerine, *vermilion* and golden yellow against a dark background of hebe, skimmia and coral fern.

59

With their blue undertones, the two varieties of red rose used for this *glamorous*, domed bouquet look particularly good in *winter*. Here, they're framed by *folded aspidistra leaves*, buffed up with a little oil for extra gleam.

This sophisticated bouquet in shades of red and burgundy has lots of *textural interest*: velvety roses, silky peonies and chenille-like *cockscomb* and *love-lies-bleeding*. Plum-coloured ribbon ties the stems.

Perfect for a *Christmas wedding*, this bouquet captures the essence of the season, with blood-red roses, *scarlet amaryllis*, winter jasmine, camellia leaves, *pine foliage*, variegated ivy and silver cones, all tied with a huge, forest-green bow.

Exuberant and *tropical*, this is a bouquet for the adventurous bride. Cool green
palm leaves frame heliconias and *ginger lilies*, looking like birds of paradise in
shades of coral, orange and pinky red.

The *rich colours of autumn* have been gathered together in this exquisite bouquet, which combines fruits, flowers and foliage – oak leaves, roses, *cape gooseberries*, hypericum berries, *kumquats* and skimmia flowers.

Tied with cream satin ribbon, this unusual little bunch of **pink-budded skimmia** and red-spotted orange **vanda orchids** shows that even the smallest and simplest of arrangements can make a strong statement.

Fun and unconventional, this bouquet is a **bold** but carefully **balanced** mixture of colours. There are lilac and purple sweet peas; *pink, orange and purple* ranunculuses; and white camellias, finished with multicoloured ribbon and burgundy net.

This lush bouquet has a collar of *variegated hosta* leaves encircling scented blue hyacinths and silky-petalled purple *gloxinias*, a flower usually sold in garden centres as a conservatory plant. *Shimmering* purple organza ribbon ties the stems.

Black and white is a daringly dramatic combination. These aubergine *calla or arum lilies* are about as close to black as flowers get and make a *sultry partner* for pure white ones, their stems tied with blades of steel grass.

This **black and white bouquet** is somewhat softer and more romantic. Black-red roses balance
white ranunculuses and poppy anemones, whose feathery centres are a true black. A ruff of
galax leaves and black-and-gold ribbon finishes the picture.

This spectacular modern arrangement of *painter's palettes*, snake grass and *aspidistra leaves* is part bouquet, part *sculpture*, thanks to the soldering wire which has been looped around the stems and over the top of the flowers.

This bouquet of mauve, gold, orange, *pale apricot* and deep red roses, framed by camellia leaves, shows how *gorgeous* unusual colour combinations can be. Fine, coloured wire has been woven over the flowers like *spun sugar*.

Contemporary Bouquets • Hot and Intense Colours

FINISHING
TOUCHES

A *wrist corsage* could take the place of a conventional bridal bouquet. Here, pristine *eucharis lilies* have been used, with individual heads pinned to long lengths of *white satin* ribbon.

This single, *perfect rose* in a shade of palest pink is a simple but stunning alternative
to a *tiara*, anchoring a waist-length tulle veil. Any *floral headdress* needs careful pinning
to ensure that it stays in place all day.

Roses are a *good choice* for headdresses because they'll stand up well to a day's celebrations and still look good at the end of the reception. These *ivory roses* have been interspersed with *variegated ivy* leaves.

The *intense reds* of this headdress look very striking against the bride's dark hair.
The *texture* of the flowers – a rose, ruffled cockscomb and tassels of *love-lies-bleeding*
– is such that they look as though they could be made from fabric.

Finishing Touches

Sweet peas in every shade of purple from lilac to *plum* have
been wired onto an Alice band to make this headdress,
carefully graduated from pale to dark shades.

This bride has chosen *seasonal flowers* for her winter wedding. A single,
flawless camellia and early-flowering clematis flowers and foliage have been
wired into a headdress which anchors a *full-length veil*.

In place of a headdress, *single florets* of green hydrangea and *soft pink roses* have been pinned into this bride's tumbling, Pre-Raphaelite curls to give a relaxed, natural look.

Far more *memorable* than a 'just married' sign, a large wreath of white *marguerites*, finished with a ribbon bow, decorates the boot of the newlyweds' car, ready for them to make a *stylish getaway*.

Flowers for the Bridesmaids

Introduction

The bridesmaids' flowers must complement the bride's but not outshine them, and it's appropriate for them to be discernibly different. They should follow the same broad colour and floral scheme, at the same time offering an interesting variation on it. For instance, if the bridal bouquet consists of white roses bound with pink satin ribbon, the bridesmaids might carry posies of pink spray roses tied with white ribbon.

Adult bridesmaids can carry bouquets or posies (it's usual for their arrangements to be smaller than the bride's), which can be complemented by hair accessories such as floral hair slides or combs. A wrist corsage makes

a stylish alternative to a traditional posy; another option is a chic bag filled with flowers (which can be taken home to keep afterwards). Young bridesmaids can be given bags or small wicker baskets to carry. They're a good practical choice: accessories and arrangements for children must be comfortable and easy to hold, ideally given to their recipients at the very last minute to avoid damage to fragile blooms. Old-fashioned charm is usually a very successful look for little girls: May Queen-style circlets; floral Alice bands; posies with ribbon streamers; hoops bound with ribbon and entwined with flowers; or floral balls finished with satin bows.

POSIES and
BOUQUETS

White is a great *foil* for other, more dramatic colours. Here, *classic white roses*
have been combined with bold touches of *deep red* in the form of freesias
and hypericum berries.

Flowers for the Bridesmaids

These ***calla or arum lilies*** are smaller and more delicate than those used for
the bridal bouquet on page 46. They look very ***elegant*** gathered into a little
sheaf with a couple of ***eucharis lilies***.

This *generous*, ribbon-tied bunch is designed to look as though it has just been
plucked from a country garden, with *lupins*, stocks, carnations and sweet peas joining
roses and even ripening *blackberries*.

This is another bunch inspired by the colourful informality of a cottage garden, mixing marguerites, *snowberries*, roses, stocks, delphiniums, *bupleurum* and freesias, all tied with *sky-blue* velvet ribbon.

When flowers are as *romantic* and beautiful as this, they deserve to be used on their own.
This bouquet of *ice-cream pink* hydrangeas and their own leaves needs nothing more than
matching satin *ribbon* to finish it.

Flowers for the Bridesmaids

This large bouquet has a ***grand air***, although the arrangement is anything but stiff and formal. ***Bronze-green*** wire-edged ribbon binds the stems of lilies, roses, kangaroo paw and ***photinia foliage*** and flowers.

This unpretentious, *cheerful* bunch of daisy-like feverfew and *golden globe flowers* shows that even commonplace plants can look glorious – just use them *generously* and finish the bouquet with pretty ribbon.

Flowers for the Bridesmaids

This bouquet encapsulates the *spirit of spring* with a refreshing palette of white, yellow and sappy green. *Gingham ribbon* ties a bunch of ranunculuses, guelder rose, spring snowflakes, senecio and various *narcissi*.

This small posy puts the focus on *colour and form*. Galax leaves frame a tight cluster of ranunculuses, their *multi-petalled heads* changing from bright orange to lime green in the centre. *Raffia* ties the stems.

Flowers for the Bridesmaids

White satin ribbon ties a small spring posy of *golden ranunculuses*, some with
green centres, and exquisite *white narcissi*, which will exude their wonderful
scent in a warm atmosphere.

These delightful posies showcase *green* in all its subtle nuances, from *apple and lime* to dark, forest greens. They use ivy, Singapore orchids, guelder rose, *hellebores*, lisianthus, laurustinus and euonymus.

This is not a colour scheme for the faint hearted, though the result is certainly stylish and *dramatic*. Black-red and *crimson* roses contrast with *lime-green* guelder rose, and the bouquet has been finished with burgundy ribbon.

Two *subtly different* varieties of red rose take centre stage in this neat, round bouquet. They are interspersed with elegantly pointed *skimmia leaves* and their buds, while *deep red ribbon* binds the stems.

Flowers for the Bridesmaids

Red roses with blue, rather than yellow, undertones – think of *ruby and burgundy*, rather than vermilion – always look particularly at home in the thin light of *winter*. This posy uses one variety, their stems bound with *dark green ribbon*.

101

This dainty posy uses flowers beloved of the Victorians, *lilies of the valley* and violets, whose delicate form and *sweet scent* ensure their enduring appeal. Two shades of thin purple ribbon and *sequinned* braid spiral round the stems.

By tradition, lily of the valley symbolizes sweetness and purity. Here, its *bell-like*, scented flowers have been framed by a *collar of ivy* leaves, while *white silk* ribbon with a dark brown edge ties the stems.

Blue is *cool and calming* and, of course, closely associated with weddings. This simple but *charming* posy of grape hyacinths and *cornflowers*, tied with navy ribbon, shows how attractive different tones of blue can look together.

Flowers for the Bridesmaids

More *sultry* than red or pink, the dramatic, *plum-purple* tones of these ranunculuses make
a very strong statement. However, a collar of snowy white *feathers* gives the arrangement
a bridal-party touch.

This floral ball is *fabulous*, frivolous and fun. Ranunculuses, pansies, cineraria and *African violets* – all in strong pinks and purples – have been wired and inserted into an oasis ball, along with feathers and *feather butterflies*.

Flowers for the Bridesmaids

An assortment of *ribbons* ties this loose bunch of lilac and *poppy anemones*.
The unstructured shape of the bouquet and the *vibrant* colours of the flowers
give the arrangement a relaxed, informal look.

HEADDRESSES

This *floral hair comb* is easy enough to make at home. Orchids last well when cut; three pink-and-white *cymbidiums* have been used here, stuck with a hot-glue gun (available from craft suppliers) to an ordinary hair comb.

Flowers for the Bridesmaids

A wide *hairslide* has been used for this gorgeous *confection* of pink and white flowers.
Blooms of similar size have been chosen – delicate spray roses and *frilly carnations* – then
carefully wired onto the comb.

For a *young bridesmaid*, nothing looks more charming than a headdress of fresh flowers.
Here, a mixture of *cottage-garden* favourites, among them roses, *cornflowers* and ivy,
have been wired onto an Alice band already dotted with tiny fabric flowers.

In the hands of a skilled florist, *pansies* are not just useful bedding plants. They have many uses for wedding flowers – here, a *sumptuous* purple variety has been wired into a *bridesmaid's circlet*.

Enchanting fabric *butterflies* have been wired onto this young bridesmaid's floral hair accessory, so that they *flutter* as she moves. They accompany *pinky-mauve* roses, green-tinged pink hydrangea florets and a base of silvery grey leaves.

Flowers for the Bridesmaids

This *verdant circlet* makes the most of the fresh greens and whites of *early-summer flowering* shrubs, with greenish white *guelder rose* heads, bridal wreath flowers and leaves, and euonymus foliage.

The *pompom-like* pink double daisies used for these headdresses can be found (along with blue and white varieties) in garden centres, sold as bedding plants. Here, however, they've been wired with ivy leaves into circlets fit for *fairies*.

Flowers for the Bridesmaids

Hydrangeas are among the few garden flowers which are *truly blue*. This variety, the colour of a cloudless *summer sky*, has been wired into thick crowns and *floral balls*, embellished with pale and dark blue ribbons.

BASKETS
and other ideas

Floral balls are time-consuming to make because flowers usually need to be *wired* before being pushed into an oasis ball, but they last well and always make an *impact*. This glowing display uses tulips, roses, *snowberries* and euonymus.

Flowers for the Bridesmaids

Another floral ball, this time in a *cooler scheme* of green, cream and white. The *hypericum* berries, roses and smaller *spray roses* used here have strong stems, so were all inserted straight into an oasis ball.

This floral ball is for those with a taste for the *unconventional*. While the shape is classic, the plants are not: *green* cymbidium orchids flecked with purple and skimmia leaves, finished with sumptuous *purple* wire-edged ribbon.

Flowers for the Bridesmaids

These young bridesmaids hold small woven *baskets* filled with miniature or patio roses
in warm shades of *sugar pink*, deep pink and golden yellow. Mint green and pale pink ribbon
streamers add to the fun.

Decorated hoops are a delight, harking back to Kate Greenaway-style images of childhood. This one has been covered in roses, **bridal wreath**, lisianthus, ivy and **euonymus**, and finished with a big white bow.

In a nod to old *customs* and rituals, these little bridesmaids carry floral *'maypoles'* – in fact, broomstick handles wrapped in ribbon, topped with posies composed of pansies, double daisies, *forget-me-nots* and columbines.

These fabulous *sequinned bags* are a more *sophisticated* way for adult bridesmaids to carry flowers and double up as presents to take home. The roses were inserted into oasis blocks, wrapped in clingfilm to keep the bags dry.

A basket of *pure white flowers* for an early summer wedding. *Moss* has been wired onto the outside of the basket and ivy twisted around the handle, before filling it with pansies and *lilies of the valley*.

Pliable *pussy willow* has been fashioned into a handle for this galvanized bucket, which
overflows with the colours of *spring* in the form of grape hyacinths, *English bluebells* and
white Spanish bluebells.

Lilac has a *wonderful sweet scent* and, despite its name, comes in whites, *pinks* and purples, as well as mauve. For this circlet, finished with *purple ribbons*, two varieties (along with skimmia leaves) create a pretty effect.

Buttonholes and Corsages

Introduction

Buttonholes are normally worn by the bridegroom, best man, ushers and fathers of the couple, and consist of a single bloom or tiny posy with a sprig of foliage. Roses and carnations are classic buttonhole choices, while for gorgeous scent you could try lily of the valley, freesias or stephanotis. Bold flowers such as calla lilies and orchids strike a modern note. Make sure that buttonholes are securely fastened, and don't forget to give someone extra pins in case there aren't enough to go round.

Corsages may be worn by the mothers and grandmothers of the couple and are the same size or a little larger than a buttonhole. Corsages are pinned onto the outfit, usually on the chest, collar, lapel or wrist. Bear in mind that, if the wearer's clothes are made of very fine fabric, the corsage should be small and light so it doesn't drag or tear. They can also be fixed with tiny magnets, one concealed in the arrangement and the other behind the dress fabric.

A *rose* buttonhole is a classic choice, but in *searing orange* it's definitely fun
rather than fusty, its brilliantly coloured petals *livening* up the dark tones
of traditional morning dress.

Buttonholes and Corsages

Presenting buttonholes to their wearers on a pretty tray is a small detail, but one of the many little things that can make the day ***special*** for all participants. Here, ***deep pink roses*** and ivy leaves lie on a tray with heart cut-out handles.

Instead of giving the men in the bridal party identical buttonholes, why not use a *range* of *complementary* flowers? From left: pink spray roses with rose leaves; *stocks* and variegated ivy; a dark red rose and ivy leaf.

With its extraordinary, sculptural shape and *intensely dark* colour, this calla lily makes
a striking buttonhole, accompanied by loops of bear grass, one of them threaded with
a *clear glass bead* for *subtle* sparkle.

Buttonholes, clockwise from top left: a rose with a ruffle of *cockscomb*, the stems bound in green ribbon; a white rose, gold-sprayed *willow catkins* and skimmia leaves; a golden rose and variegated euonymus; a rose, winter jasmine and a bow of *cranberry* ribbon.

Buttonholes and Corsages

Clockwise from top left: grape hyacinths, *galax leaves* and narrow navy ribbon; a pink *parrot tulip* and its leaf; sprigs of rosemary and copper-brown *striped ribbon*; scented hyacinth florets and navy ribbon.

Buttonholes, clockwise from top left: a rose, *hydrangea florets* and ivy, their stems spiral bound with two colours of narrow ribbon; viburnum flowers and foliage; a *moth orchid*, camellia leaves and grosgrain ribbon; a burnt-orange gerbera with *turquoise* and lime-green ribbon.

Buttonholes, from left: *lilac buds* with white ribbon and braid; a stem of ivy with *royal purple* ribbon; *aromatic* rosemary and dove-grey ribbon; exotic kangaroo paw and moss-green ribbon.

Grey-green narrow *velvet* ribbon tightly binds the stems of this buttonhole
of white rosebuds and white *heather* (which, traditionally, is supposed to
bring *good luck* to the wearer).

Cream velvet ribbon has been bound around the stems of this buttonhole – composed
of irises, *freesias* and *mimosa* – in a distinctive criss-cross pattern, showing that, even
on a small scale, there is always room for *inventiveness*.

Corsages, clockwise from top left: fragrant sweet peas, wired beads and sequinned trim;
a rose, ivy leaf and *rosebud braid*; globe flowers, feverfew and a galax leaf;
scented white narcissi and dark green *ruched ribbon*.

This *classic corsage* has been wired to keep it light – particularly important if it's to be worn on an outfit made of delicate fabric. It's composed of freesias, *hypericum berries*, a rose, a large ivy leaf and *jasmine*.

This *elegant* corsage of white spray roses, stephanotis buds and
variegated ivy has been injected with a bit of fun by tying the stems
with *polka-dot satin* ribbon.

Buttonholes and Corsages

For an *evening reception*, give adult bridesmaids a *glamorous* little sequinned bag
full of flowers in place of a traditional corsage. Here, pansies have been chosen for their
velvety petals and intense colour.

A wrist corsage is an unusual and *stylish variation* on the corsage theme.
Here, a head of hydrangea, its petals white *tinged with green*, has been
pinned to a length of pretty floral braid.

Buttonholes and Corsages

This *cymbidium* orchid is a practical as well as beautiful choice for a wrist corsage – orchids *last well* when cut. It's been attached with a hot-glue gun (from craft suppliers) to wide ribbon.

Flowers for the Reception

Introduction

The bride and bridesmaids' bouquets set the tone for the
flowers at the reception, such as table centrepieces, chair-
back decorations, favours and decorations for the cake.
However, the surroundings also help to determine the
style of the reception displays. Important considerations
include the level of formality or informality; whether the
reception is indoors or out; whether the room's decor is
traditional or modern and so on.

Whatever style you adopt, the table arrangements
mustn't detract from the main business of the day, which
is eating, drinking, talking and having fun. Towering
centrepieces will impede the flow of conversation. Guests
should be able to see over or through arrangements easily,
and remember that beautifully scented flowers will
enhance their enjoyment of the celebrations.

Think creatively about the containers you use, whether you choose vases, bowls, galvanized buckets, terracotta pots or even goldfish bowls. Oasis rings can be turned into spectacular floral wreaths to display on walls, doors or tables. You could add candles to some of your displays, particularly if the reception is an evening one. If you want to give your guests floral favours to take home as mementoes, these could be used as part of the table decorations, perhaps doubling up as name-card holders at each place setting. Flowers can transform the humblest of venues but since they will have served their purpose by the end of the reception, encourage guests to take arrangements home with them. While you're on your honeymoon, they'll be enjoying your wedding flowers at home.

153

TABLE CENTREPIECES

This linear arrangement of *eucalyptus*, roses, carnations, *hypericum berries*, loosestrife and bear grass, all in *cooling shades* of white, cream and green, has been designed with a long, rectangular table in mind.

A white and green scheme again, but this time *modern and exotic* in feel. The display features limes (brushed with petroleum jelly to prevent discolouration), chrysanthemums, *roses*, painter's palettes and *variegated foliage*.

An oasis ring is the base for this *romantic arrangement*. It uses salal foliage, hydrangeas, roses, freesias, lisianthus and *veronicas*, with a *chunky candle* in the centre to cast a warm glow over the table.

A square glass vase houses this pretty display of roses, their *full-blown* heads interspersed with stems of *senecio* foliage. A simple centrepiece such as this relies on using *perfect blooms* in quantity to achieve its effect.

159

This centrepiece, an abundant display of roses, *crab apples*, snowberries, bupleurum and jasmine in a *galvanized bucket*, has been designed to give a *country-garden feel* to an outdoor reception.

Another *al fresco* table setting, this time more formal and sophisticated. The fine china and crystal are complemented by a shallow *silver bowl* filled with pink spray roses, *scented stephanotis* and variegated ivy.

Red, white and green are an *ideal combination* for a winter wedding.
The carnations in this centrepiece are *richest ruby* and make a pleasing
foil for the *pure white* stephanotis and variegated ivy.

A *simple white pot* has been dressed up by placing it on folded satin ribbon. In it have been placed roses in an exquisite shade of *apricot*, with extra *petals* scattered down the length of the table.

This goldfish bowl makes an unexpected but *magnificent* centrepiece. A huge,
ice-cream pink peony, pink-and-white rose and magenta Singapore orchid float
inside, surrounded by more *peonies*, roses and orchids.

A joyous display of cottage-garden favourites — lupins, stocks, carnations, sweet peas, roses, ripening *blackberries* and cow parsley — seems to erupt from a tall, *fluted glass* vase at this late-summer wedding in the country.

Many **bulbs** burst into glorious life in spring and this centrepiece features two
highly scented ones – **hyacinths** (here in indigo) and narcissi (a variety called
Paperwhite) – in a simple, painted terracotta pot.

This delightful centrepiece also displays a *table number*, combining practicality with beauty. The painted terracotta pot, finished with a sash of ribbon, has been planted with *scented jasmine*, trained over a hoop.

167

Table Centrepieces

Elegant, *slender tapers* emerge from a *cloud* of white cow parsley and
nerines to make a display of ethereal beauty. Since tapers don't have a
long burning time, don't light them until the meal is about the start.

This table setting has a ***grand and formal*** air, created by using fine china, crystal and *silverware*. An antique silver urn, filled with roses, tulips, mimosa, *snowberries* and senecio, is a magnificent centrepiece.

CHAIRS and
PLACE SETTINGS

An artificial wreath with *tiny blue* fabric roses has been used as a base for this
circlet, hung *casually* over the back of a chair. *Fresh mimosa* has been added for
a splash of cheerful yellow.

Flowers for the Reception

This posy of *laurel*, senecio, tulips, roses and snowberries has been
tied to its chair with white ribbon and, with the addition of
a *handwritten tag*, also acts as a place marker.

A simple white folding chair has been gorgeously decorated for an outdoor reception.
Hosta leaves frame *pinky red roses*, white-and-pink spray roses, carnations and
stephanotis buds, all tied with *green ribbon*.

Flowers for the Reception

Two *spectacular* chair decorations mark the ***bride and groom's places*** at top
table. Mimosa flowers and foliage, roses, euonymus and snowberries have been
finished with a *cascade* of variegated ivy.

175

This bunch of country flowers, tied with palest *apricot ribbon*, anchors one end of a *jasmine swag* on a wide wooden bench. The arrangement includes roses, freesias, crab apples, veronicas and *Michaelmas daisies*.

Flowers for the Reception

This decoration would be ideal for the ***top table***, or just the bride and groom's chairs.
A combination of salal foliage, lilies, ***bells of Ireland***, roses and ***jasmine***, it's firmly tied
on with twine, which is then disguised with wide ribbon.

A *twig wreath* (available from florists) can easily be dressed up with *fresh flowers*. Here,
ivy has been twined around the wreath and *shocking pink* anemones wired on before
it was secured to a chair with bright pink ribbon.

Flowers for the Reception

The base for this decoration is, again, a twig wreath, which has here been attached to a wall above a seating plan with **narrow ribbon**. Variegated ivy creates an attractive **backdrop** for pink spray roses and scented **stephanotis**.

This *simple treatment* for a painted wooden chair has plenty of *country charm*. A bow
of wide, lilac satin ribbon hides the join between two bunches of *aromatic lavender*,
tied end to end.

180

This just-opened **hydrangea head**, tied to a chair with pale blue ribbon, is beautifully *soft* in colour. The idea could be recreated for next to nothing if the flowers were harvested from the **gardens** of family and friends.

Sprigs of *frothy cow parsley* and euonymus *spill out* from a dainty cone, made
at home from nothing more expensive than stiff white paper. Ribbon glued
to the back of the cone attaches it to the chair.

Flowers for the Reception

A large wreath, attached to a wall, door or window frame, is an instant *focal point*.
Here, an oasis ring is the foundation for a display of *hydrangea heads*, small pink roses,
and *wired sequins* and butterflies.

Chairs and Place Settings

This napkin-ring decoration consists of a **white freesia**, pink veronica, **skimmia leaf** and skimmia buds, all wired to keep the arrangement neat and light. A sash of **moss-green velvet ribbon** finishes the look.

Coloured *Moroccan tea glasses* are the perfect size for *small posies* (here, sweet peas,
a rose and greenish-white *guelder rose*) and make a decorative memento to be taken
home after the wedding.

Chairs and Place Settings

This pretty favour also acts as a *place-card holder*. A plain terracotta pot has been painted white, then potted up with lily of the valley, whose ***bell-like flowers*** are sweetly scented, and top dressed with moss.

This simple but stunning table setting relies on *attention to detail*. Deep, pinky red is
a dramatic *accent colour* against white, picked out by the glassware, plate rims and
rose heads which lie on each pristine napkin.

Napkin decorations, clockwise from top left: a ***wintry sprig*** of berried ivy, tied with twine; a bunch of lavender with a sash of ***sheer lilac*** ribbon; an aspidistra leaf, tied with ***bear grass***; crab apples and narrow olive-green ribbon.

Clockwise from top left: a folded napkin, decorated with a pink *scabious*, holds a place card; ribbon secures cow parsley and euonymus; *napkin holders* of wide, grey ribbon, with guests' names attached, secure rosemary sprigs; a pink lisianthus is tucked under *oyster-coloured* ribbon.

Chairs and Place Settings

FLOWERS
for the CAKE

Sophisticated and *modern*, this cake's three tiers have been simply decorated with *opalescent* icing 'pearls'. A cluster of flawless, white *eucharis lilies* on the top tier is the only extra embellishment.

Square tiers, iced in a basketweave pattern, take the place of round ones to make this glorious cake. The three tiers overflow with *full-blown roses* in subtle shades of *palest pink*, apricot, cream and white.

Hypericum berries and *pink bouvardia* have been made into posies, then fixed to each tier of this cake by pushing a pin through their bound stems. More bouvardia, cut very short, forms the domed *cake topper*.

This highly romantic and very *elegant* cake consists of four stacked tiers, decorated with graduated icing 'pearls'. Posies of ice-cream pink hydrangeas, stephanotis and *snowberries* complete the pretty picture.

Flowers for the Cake

A thoroughly *feminine* cake for a late-summer wedding: the tiers have been covered
in *blush-pink icing* and a simple piped design, then finished with individual
florets from a pink hydrangea.

Green and white is always a calming and *refreshing* combination. Here, tiny sprigs
of *bupleurum*, whose frothy flower heads are *lime green*, lend their
discreet charm to a simple cake.

The tiers of this cake have been simply iced with a tiny, ***all-over pattern***, then dressed
with luscious, pinky red roses, ***white-and-pink*** spray roses, aromatic lavender and
glossy galax leaves.

Gleaming frills decorate this elaborate, *indulgent* chocolate cake. Large *poppy anemones* in vivid shades of red, pink and purple, partnered by *sage leaves*, stand out boldly against the dark background.

FLOWERS
as FAVOURS

This miniature galvanized bucket holds a ***modest but charming*** display of cow parsley and ***euonymus***. White ***tissue paper*** lines the container, kept dry by an inner waterproofing layer of plastic.

A cluster of white *spray roses*, some fully open and some *still in bud* so that
they will continue to give a display once a guest takes the favour home, sits
in an elegant *silver pot*.

This galvanized bucket, complete with diminutive *gardener's fork*, has been planted
up with *grape hyacinths*, whose dainty, *intensely blue* flowers appear in the spring.
It does double duty as a place-card holder.

Small *terracotta* pots are inexpensive and easy to turn into decorative favours. This one has been sprayed silver and filled with an unusual combination of sea holly, whose *steel-blue cones* are surrounded by *silvery* bracts, and senecio.

205

This wicker basket, its handle decorated with a bow of *cobalt-blue* ribbon, has been filled with stem upon stem of *fragrant bluebells*, ready to be tied into posies for wedding guests.

Flowers for the Reception

With its *glorious scent* and delightful flowers, lavender's a *star plant*. Here, small
bunches of dried lavender, the stems stripped of their grey-green leaves, have been tied
with sheer white ribbon to be *handed out* to guests.

Planning

Flower checklist

Bride's bouquet

Bouquets or posies for the bridesmaids

Corsages for the mothers

Buttonholes for the groom, best man,
 ushers and fathers

Arrangements for the church or civil venue

Arrangements for the reception

Suggested colour themes

Single-colour schemes – all white, for instance – are one possibility. However, they can look monotonous, so blend deeper and paler shades of one colour for variety and remember the value of foliage.

Combining colours is the other option. A colour wheel is a visual way of dividing up the spectrum and a useful tool since it shows which colours create contrasting partnerships and which are harmonious. Opposite or contrasting pairs include red (or pink) and green; blue and yellow; purple and orange. Harmonious pairings include pink and purple; blue and green; yellow and orange. In general, dark or very bright colours need the most skilful handling; pastels are easier to use.

White is associated with purity and serenity. Ivory and cream are often more flattering than pure white, and white flowers usually have undertones – yellow, pink, blue or green – that warm or cool them. White is an ideal foil for other colours and can be combined with any of them.

Yellows can be cool or warm, and the two don't mix well. Greenish yellows blend well with green, cream, white or soft blue; golden yellows are a good match for oranges and warm reds.

Orange can be a challenge. As apricot, peach and buff it's easier to use, mixed with cream or buttery yellow. Intense orange combines well with warm yellow, gold, terracotta or warm reds; or it can be cooled with blue, green or purple.

Red is the most powerful primary colour. The addition of green, white or cream helps to tone it down. Blue reds can be mixed with reddish purples; even pink can be used with red, but only with great care.

Pink is feminine and romantic. Avoid mixing cool pinks with blue undertones and warm pinks with yellow undertones. Pink and green is a classic combination; cool pinks look beautiful with purple, blue and silver; coral can be combined with oranges and pinky reds for tropical sizzle.

Purple ranges from lilac and mauve to plum and almost black. Deep purples work with dark reds, blues or pinks for a jewel-like effect. Paler shades look good with soft blues and pale pinks. Dark purples with red undertones can be partnered with orange.

Blue ranges from true blues to purplish shades such as lavender. It blends well with white, cream, cool pink and purple; true blue works well with yellow.

Green is an invaluable partner for other colours and foliage plays a key part in most floral displays. Lime or apple greens look good with white, cream, blue and yellow; contrasting green with red, pink or purple can also be very effective.

Flower buying and care tips

- A commercial flower food will prolong the life of cut flowers. Sugar, lemonade or aspirin added to the water will also keep flowers healthier for longer.

- If you're using flowers from your own garden, they may not last as long as commercially grown flowers. Garden flowers, like bought flowers, should stand in fresh water before use.

- Make sure that any containers used for soaking flowers are clean and bacteria-free. Rinse them with water containing a little bleach before using.

- Look for bright yellow stamens on lilies; old lilies (of all varieties) have dark stamens.

- Make sure lily stamens are removed; their pollen stains anything it touches bright orange.

- Spray table arrangements with water to keep them fresh and the oasis moist.

- Keep all finished arrangements somewhere cool and dark, but don't be tempted to store any flowers, including buttonholes and corsages, in the fridge.

- The length of a teardrop bouquet should be tailored to the height of the bride: the taller the bride, the longer the bouquet can be. For a petite bride, a tied bunch is probably more flattering.

- For pinning buttonholes to lapels, buy pearl-headed pins, which look more special than normal dressmaking pins.

- Some of the longest-lasting flowers are chrysanthemums, carnations, orchids, roses, tulips and calla lilies. Sweet peas and poppy anemones, though beautiful, have a short life once cut.

- Prices of exotic flowers such as callas and orchids can rise markedly during the peak wedding months (May to July), or if supplies are low. If you're on a budget, go for flowers less prone to fluctuations in price, such as roses and carnations.

Working with a florist

When you're looking for a florist, begin by asking friends for recommendations. Your caterer or reception venue may also have some ideas. Otherwise, make appointments with several local florists. Ask if they have a portfolio, so you can see whether you like their work. Look for someone who is helpful, sympathetic to your requests, has plenty of ideas and is easy to get on with.

If possible, take along fabric swatches or pictures of your dress and your attendants' outfits, since they're the natural starting point for choosing a colour scheme. If you've been inspired by books or magazines, take these along, particularly if you don't know the names of the flowers you like. Look at flowers in the shop and don't be afraid to ask what they are if you're unsure.

Tell your florist what your budget is. Remember that the more complicated and time-consuming the arrangement (such as wired bouquets, floral 'trees', garlands or floral arches), the more expensive it is. Discuss what props you might want (vases, candelabra, pedestals) and ask who will do the arranging on the day. If the florist is unfamiliar with the venues you're using, ask if they will visit them to help you both decide what sort of arrangements you need. Failing that, show them photographs.

Once you've decided what you want, get a written estimate. Find out when the flowers will be delivered and give someone the task of being there to receive them. Ask for bouquets to be labelled, so there isn't any confusion about which is which.

Flowers for all seasons

Nowadays, many flowers are imported and so available all year round. Examples include alstroemeria, carnations, chrysanthemums, freesias, gerberas, gypsophila, lilies, orchids and roses. If you'd like to incorporate a seasonal element into your floral displays, try some of the following.

Spring Anemones, bluebells, camellias, crocuses, forget-me-nots, grape hyacinths, hyacinths, lilies of the valley, narcissi, pansies, ranunculuses, tulips, violets.

Summer Campanulas, cornflowers, delphiniums, hydrangeas, gypsophila, jasmine, lady's mantle, larkspurs, marguerites, peonies, phlox, roses, scabious, stocks, sweet peas.

Autumn Amaranthus, chrysanthemums, cosmos, dahlias, hydrangeas, Japanese anemones, Michaelmas daisies, scabious.

Winter Heather, hellebores, irises, primulas, snowdrops, winter jasmine.

Flower directory

Agapanthus (*Agapanthus*)
Summer flowers with tall stems and large heads of blue or white bell-shaped blooms. Good for adding height to arrangements.

Allium (*Allium*)
Globe-headed purple flowers that can make a wonderful impact in big displays. Good for adding blue tones to an arrangement. Alliums can smell of onions when they are going over.

Asparagus fern (*Asparagus densiflorus*)
An exceptionally delicate and feathery fern, suitable for romantic arrangements and softening the outline of a bouquet.

Aspidistra (*Aspidistra*)
Large, smooth, glossy dark green leaves that can make a bouquet 'collar'.

Bells of Ireland (*Molucella*)
Tall stems of unusual green flowers, which can exude a minty aroma.

Bluebell (*Hyacinthoides non-scripta*)
Traditional spring favourite found in many gardens (do not pick from the wild).

Bouvardia (*Bouvardia*)
An excellent bridal flower available in pink, mauve and white.

Calla or arum lily (*Zantedeschia aethiopica*)
Dramatic, sculptural blooms; expensive in the summer months.

Camellia (*Camellia*)
Flowers are white, pink or red, while the leaves are dark, glossy and very attractive. Camellia flowers are useful for winter weddings as an alternative to roses, while the hardy leaves are perfect for wiring and using in buttonholes.

Carnation (*Dianthus*)
Long lasting, excellent value and available in a huge colour range. Popular for buttonholes. Also known as pinks.

Chrysanthemum (*Chrysanthemum*)
Exceptionally long lasting and very good value for money. Available in a variety of colours and forms, including the spidery shamrock chrysanthemum.

Cornflower (*Centaurea cyanus*)
A true blue flower – relatively rare in the flower world. Synonymous with summer in the countryside.

Cow parsley (*Anthriscus sylvestris*)
Delicate white flowers found in every country lane, but also grown commercially.

Daffodil (*Narcissus*)
Quintessential spring flowers in colours from white to deep yellow. Many of the miniature varieties are scented.

Eucalyptus (*Eucalyptus*)
Attractive foliage with small, aromatic, grey-green globular leaves.

Eucharis lily (*Eucharis*)
Exceptionally elegant white flowers.

Euonymus (*Euonymus*)
Attractive foliage found in many back gardens. The leaves can be variegated with white or gold and some varieties produce pink or red autumn colour.

Forget-me-not (*Myosotis*)
Unpretentious, very pretty blue and pink flowers found in many gardens. Flowers prolifically all spring.

Freesia (*Freesia*)
Good value scented flowers on arching stems, which can provide extra shape to an arrangement. They come in many colours.

Galax (*Galax*)
Large, glossy green leaves.

Ginger lily (*Alpinia*)
Tropical, colourful flowers. Expensive but striking and dramatic, they would be ideal for a non-traditional ceremony.

Glory lily (*Gloriosa superba*)
Exotic red blooms edged with gold.

Grape hyacinth (*Muscari*)
Synonymous with spring, in colours from pale to deep blue. Useful for reception table pots and decorations.

Guelder rose (*Viburnum opulus*)
Pompom-like white blooms from a shrub found in many gardens.

Heliconia (*Heliconia*)
Sculptural tropical blooms in spicy colours.

Hellebore (*Helleborus*)
Winter flowering and so useful for winter weddings. Subtly beautiful flowers in green, pink to deep purple, and white.

Hosta (*Hosta*)
Large glossy leaves, often variegated and available in many shades of green. Useful for table arrangements.

Hyacinth (*Hyacinthus*)
Highly scented, they are useful for table decorations and come in a good colour range from white to yellow, blue, pink and purple.

Hydrangea (*Hydrangea*)
Useful for late summer and early autumn colour, the huge flower heads come in white, pink, blue, mauve, lime green and even red.

Hypericum (*Hypericum*)
Green, orange and cream berried foliage. Very useful for filling gaps in arrangements. Also known as St John's Wort.

Iceland poppy (*Papaver croceum*)
Available in white, yellow and burnt orange. Before using, condition the cut stems by singeing with a match.

Iris (*Iris*)
Both winter and summer flowering varieties are available, in a huge colour range, often white, yellow, blue and purple.

Ivy (*Hedera helix*)
Ivy is found in many gardens, but can also be purchased. Comes in many variegated forms as well as plain green.

Jasmine (*Jasminum*)
There are winter and summer jasmines.

Lady's mantle (*Alchemilla mollis*)
The frothy lime-green flowers are a very useful foil for other flower colours.

Lavender (*Lavandula*)
Useful for adding scent to a bouquet or table arrangement.

Lily (*Lilium*)
Spectacular large flowers that make a real impact in a bouquet, in many colours. Many varieties are highly scented.

Lily of the valley (*Convallaria majalis*)
A traditional wedding favourite, beautifully scented. The small, delicate flowers are best suited to a small posy or a table arrangement.

Lisianthus (*Eustoma*)
The flowers, often in white, lilac or pink, are reminiscent of roses. Good value.

Loosestrife (*Lysimachia*)
Some types sparse in summer. Long, elegant tapered flowers, useful as vertical accents.

Lupin (*Lupinus*)
Cottage-garden favourites. Tall and dramatic, they are available in a wide colour range.

Marguerite (*Argyranthemum frutescens*)
Cheerful white daisy-like flowers, ideal for summer weddings.

Michaelmas daisy (*Aster novi-belgii*)
Useful for late summer and autumn colour, usually in whites, pinks and purples.

Orchid
This large family of flowers includes the varieties **Singapore orchids** (*Dendrobium*), **cymbidium** and **moth orchids** (*Phalaenopsis*). They are expensive, but make excellent wedding flowers; they are available in a wide choice of shades, extremely long-lasting and exquisite. Even if used sparingly, they will still make an impact.

Painter's palette (*Anthurium*)
Impressive sculptural blooms that bruise very easily.

Peony (*Paeonia*)
The first true flowers of summer. Huge, blowsy flowers in colours ranging from white to deep pink, sometimes scented. The pale pink Sarah Bernhardt variety lasts well.

Poppy anemone (*Anemone coronaria De Caen*)
Large, open flowers with bold black centres, in blue, pink, red and white.

Ranunculus (*Ranunculus*)

Beautiful, tightly furled flowers in an unusual colour range.

Rose (*Rosa*)

A very good all-round flower for all kinds of wedding arrangements, available in myriad colours. There are small-flowered spray roses as well as large varieties. Bear in mind that commercially grown roses are usually scentless.

Scabious (*Scabiosa*)

Pretty summer and early autumn flowers in pastel shades.

Skimmia (*Skimmia*)

A useful foliage shrub for all sorts of arrangements, with dark green leaves and white flowers. If you want the red berries, they are available in winter only. The leaves are good used in buttonholes with smaller rose varieties.

Snapdragon (*Antirrhinum*)

Cottage-garden favourite in a wide range of pretty, bright colours.

Stephanotis (*Stephanotis floribunda*)

Exquisite, scented, white waxy flowers that begin as decorative buds.

Stock (*Matthiola*)

Traditional country-garden flowers, in pretty pastels including white, pink and lilac. They are usually scented and are good value.

Sweet pea (*Lathyrus odoratus*)

Not very long lasting, but beautiful flowers in a huge range of colours including white, purple, pink and sometimes red. Well known for their perfume, but commercially grown varieties are not always scented.

Tulip (*Tulipa*)

Long-lasting, good-value flowers in a huge range of colours and forms, including ruffled and striped varieties.

Veronica (*Veronica*)

Elegant, tapering spires of flowers, usually in white, purple or pink. Useful as a contrasting form to round flowers.

Flower matching chart

SCHEME: **Fresh white and green**

BRIDE

p17 Bouquet of peonies, roses, dill and bridal wreath

BRIDAL PARTY

p115 Bridesmaid's circlet of guelder rose, bridal wreath and euonymus

p124 Bridesmaid's hoop of roses, bridal wreath, lisianthus, ivy and euonymus

• Try rose or lisianthus buttonholes with ivy or euonymus for foliage

RECEPTION

p168 Table centrepiece of cow parsley and nerines or try arrangements of peonies, roses, guelder rose, bridal wreath, ivy and euonymus

p182 Chair back of cow parsley and euonymus

p189 Top right, napkin decoration of cow parsley and euonymus

p197 Cake with bupleurum

p202 Favour of cow parsley with euonymus

SCHEME: **Classic white**

BRIDE

p18 Bouquet of roses, loosestrife, lilac and eucalyptus

BRIDAL PARTY

p121 Bridesmaid's ball of roses and hypericum berries

p145 Corsage of rose, hypericum berries, freesias, ivy and jasmine

• Try buttonholes of white spray roses and green hypericum berries

RECEPTION

p156 Table centrepiece of roses, carnations, hypericum berries, loosestrife, bear grass and eucalyptus

p167 Table centrepiece of white jasmine

p203 Favour of white spray roses

• Try chair decorations of white or cream roses, lime-green carnations and eucalyptus

SCHEME: Romantic pink

BRIDE

p23   Bouquet of roses, stocks and freesias

BRIDAL PARTY

p111   Hair accessory of spray roses and carnations

p126   Bridesmaid's bags filled with roses

•   Try bridesmaids' posies of white, cream and pink roses and carnations, and buttonholes of smaller, spray roses in the same colours

RECEPTION

p158   Table centrepiece of hydrangeas, roses, freesias, lisianthus, veronica and salal

p183   Wreath of roses and hydrangeas

p195   Cake decoration of hydrangea, stephanotis and snowberries

•   Try chair decorations of pink roses and lisianthus, and white freesias

SCHEME: Summer in the garden

BRIDE

•   Try a larger version of the bridesmaid's bouquet, with lupins, roses, stocks, carnations, sweet peas and blackberries

BRIDAL PARTY

p90   Bridesmaid's bouquet of lupins, roses, stocks, carnations, sweet peas and blackberries

p111   Hair accessory of spray roses and carnations

p135   Rose buttonholes

RECEPTION

p165   Table centrepiece of lupins, roses, stocks, sweet peas, blackberries, carnations and cow parsley

p174   Chair back of roses, carnations, stephanotis and hosta leaves

p198   Cake decoration of roses, lavender and galax leaves

•   Try favours of pale and deep pink spray roses in floral tea or coffee cups

SCHEME: **True blue**

BRIDE	BRIDAL PARTY	RECEPTION
p30 Bouquet of hydrangeas, delphiniums, sea holly and ivy	p117 Bridesmaids' hydrangea circlets and balls • Try hydrangea posies for the bridesmaids and buttonholes of wired hydrangea florets or cornflowers	• Try table centrepieces of delphiniums, hydrangeas and sea holly, with hydrangea florets on the cake similar to p195 p181 Hydrangea chair decoration • Try napkin decorations of delphinium and hydrangea florets

SCHEME: **Sweet lilac**

BRIDE	BRIDAL PARTY	RECEPTION
p31 Bouquet of white and mauve lilac p43 Bouquet of lilac and poppy anemones	p107 Bridesmaid's bouquet of lilac and poppy anemones p129 Bridesmaid's circlet of lilac and skimmia • Try poppy anemone buttonholes	• Try centrepieces of white and mauve lilac and a cake decoration of poppy anemones • Try decorating chair backs with lilac heads tied on with purple ribbon, similar to p180 or 181

SCHEME: **Winter reds**

BRIDE	BRIDAL PARTY	RECEPTION
p38 Bouquet of roses, senecio and galax p60 Bouquet of roses and aspidistra p62 Bouquet of roses, amaryllis and jasmine	p100 Bridesmaid's bouquet of roses and skimmia p101 Bridesmaid's bouquet of roses • Try red rose buttonholes	• Try table centrepieces with red roses and amaryllis, and dark evergreen foliage, with candles if the reception goes on after dark. Decorate the cake with red roses and jasmine

SCHEME: Modern white

BRIDE

p24 Bouquet of calla lilies

p46 Bouquet of calla lilies
and bear grass

BRIDAL PARTY

p89 Bridesmaid's posy of calla
lilies and eucharis lilies

• Try white calla lily
buttonholes similar to p137

RECEPTION

p157 Table centrepiece of
painter's palettes, limes,
carnations and roses

• Try placing long-stemmed
calla lilies in tall glass vases

SCHEME: Elegant simplicity

BRIDE

p51 Bouquet of eucharis lilies

p74 Wrist corsage of
eucharis lilies

• Try pinning single eucharis
lilies in the bride's hair

BRIDAL PARTY

p89 Bridesmaid's posy of calla
lilies and eucharis lilies

RECEPTION

• Try clear glass vases
filled with long-stemmed
eucharis lilies

p192 Cake decoration of
eucharis lilies

SCHEME: Golden wedding

BRIDE

p52 Bouquet of tulips

BRIDAL PARTY

p120 Bridesmaid's ball of tulips,
roses and snowberries

p138 Bottom right, rose
buttonhole

RECEPTION

p169 Table centrepiece of
roses, tulips, snowberries,
mimosa and senecio

p173 Chair back of laurel,
senecio, roses, tulips
and snowberries

p175 Chair back of roses,
mimosa, snowberries,
ivy and euonymus

• Try golden spray roses
on the cake

Ribbons and accessories

Flowers are the stars of any bouquet but, just as the right accessories can make an outfit, finishing an arrangement with gorgeous trimmings heightens its beauty.

Ribbon is incredibly useful for this because it comes in so many different finishes, fabrics, patterns and colours. Even the simplest bunched posy can be given a bridal look by finishing it with a pretty bow. Go for a browse around a good haberdashery department to see the different types on offer: satin and taffeta (which can be plain or patterned, with a plain or decorative edge); sheer (these can sometimes be 'shot' for extra shimmer); grosgrain (which has a distinctive ribbed texture); jacquard (with a woven, rather than printed, pattern); velvet; wire edged; metallic; pleated and ruched.

Ribbon can be used to bind the stems of a bouquet or posy completely (see page 41), which looks decorative and serves the useful practical purpose of making it more comfortable to hold for a long time. Alternatively, ribbon can be used just to tie the stems under the head of the bouquet (see page 42), finishing in a bow. A good florist should be able to arrange ribbon into various sorts of bows, some with multiple loops for an extravagant look (see page 54). Wide, wire-edged ribbons are particularly useful for

bouquets because they keep their shape so well when fashioned into a bow.

There's no reason to limit yourself to one type of ribbon, of course, and very pretty effects can be created by layering sheer and satin ribbon; or combining wide and narrow ribbons; or ribbons in different shades (see page 29). Sheer fabrics such as organza and net can also be used to create a 'collar' around a bouquet (see pages 37 and 50), and fine tulle can be used to envelop a bouquet for an ultra-romantic, soft-focus look (see page 49). Leaving ribbon ends long can create a more dramatic look (see page 24) and adding ribbon streamers to a bouquet (see page 32) gives it a more traditional, rustic look. Narrow ribbon, braid and other trimmings

are useful for finishing buttonholes and corsages, and although these arrangements are on a small scale, there is plenty of scope for creativity in the way the stems are decorated (see pages 140 to 141).

The usual way to secure ribbon to the stem of a bouquet is with pearl-headed pins, which can themselves be further decorated by threading beads onto them (see page 26). Beads, wired beads or sequins can be used for glamorous sparkle, perhaps threaded onto fine grasses (see page 46), or tucked in amongst flowers (see page 23). Artificial butterflies can be wired and used alongside flowers (see pages 106 and 183), as can feathers (see page 105). In a much more contemporary vein, sculptural effects can

be created by using wire to bind stems and encircle bouquets (see pages 58 and 70). Very fine wire can be worked into a lattice to give a lighter effect, not unlike spun sugar (see page 71).

Paint may sound like an unlikely ingredient in floristry, but sprays have their uses. In winter, bare branches, twigs and dried seed heads can be transformed with metallic spray paint. Flowers, too, can be sprayed but, for the best effect, this needs to be done very lightly, so that the petals are merely touched with colour. Another unusual technique is to mist flowers with spray adhesive (from art suppliers), then apply glitter. All these effects work best on flowers which have a good shape and petals that aren't too flimsy, such as roses.

The language of flowers

It is believed that the idea of associating meanings or sentiments with particular flowers was introduced to Europe from Asia in the eighteenth century. However, it was the Victorians who popularized the idea in this country, allowing through flowers the expression of emotions which couldn't be voiced openly in polite society. It may add to your enjoyment of the flowers you choose for your wedding to know that they have a special meaning.

Alstroemeria . . . . *Friendship*
Amaryllis . . . . *Splendid beauty*
Calla lily . . . . *Delicacy*
Camellia . . . . *Perfect beauty*
Carnation . . . . *Pure and deep love; woman's love*
Cherry blossom . . . . *Spiritual beauty*
Chrysanthemum . . . . *Truth*
Chrysanthemum, red . . . . *In love*

Cornflower	*Delicacy*
Crocus	*Youthful gladness; cheerfulness*
Daffodil	*Regard*
Dahlia	*Forever thine*
Daisy	*Innocence*
Daisy, double	*Enjoyment*
Freesia	*Innocence*
Gardenia	*Ecstasy*
Guelder rose	*Age*
Gypsophila	*Fruitful marriage*
Heather, white	*Good luck*
Honeysuckle	*Fidelity; the band of love*
Hyacinth	*Constancy*
Hyacinth, white	*Unobtrusive loveliness*
Iris	*A message*
Ivy	*Matrimony*
Lavender	*Love and devotion*
Lilac, purple	*First emotions of love*
Lilac, white	*Youth*
Lily	*Purity; modesty*

Lily of the valley . . . . *Return of happiness*

Mallow . . . . *Sweetness; good and kind*

Marjoram . . . . *Blushes*

Mimosa . . . . *Modesty; delicate feelings*

Orchid . . . . *A belle*

Palm . . . . *Victory*

Pansy . . . . *You occupy my thoughts*

Pansy, yellow . . . . *Think of me*

Peony . . . . *Happy marriage*

Periwinkle . . . . *Sweet memories*

Phlox . . . . *United hearts*

Polyanthus . . . . *Confidence*

Primrose . . . . *Eternal youth*

Ranunculus . . . . *Radiant with charms*

Rose . . . . *Love; beauty*

Rose, blush . . . . *If you love me, you will find it out*

Rose, cabbage . . . . *Ambassador of love*

Rose, full blown . . . . *You are beautiful*

Rose, full white . . . . *I am worthy of you*

Rose, red . . . . *I love you*

Rosebud . . . . *Youth*

Snowdrop . . . . *A friend in adversity*

Stock . . . . *Lasting beauty*

Sunflower . . . . *Adoration*

Sweet pea . . . . *Departure*

Tulip . . . . *Fame*

Veronica . . . . *Fidelity*

Violet . . . . *Modesty*

Source list

Flowers

The Flowers and Plants Association
www.flowers.org.uk
A website with helpful sections such as what's in flower when and choosing flowers for colour and scent. It also lists florists in the UK.

These websites will help you to find florists nationwide:
www.flowershopsuk.com
www.webflorists.co.uk

Ribbon

Hobbycraft
0800 0272387
www.hobbycraft.co.uk
Stores nationwide and mail order. Has a special wedding section which sells floral sundries, ribbon, corsages and other items.

John Lewis
Oxford Street
London W1A 1EX
020 7629 7711
www.johnlewis.com

Call 08456 049049 or visit the website for branches nationwide. Haberdashery, ready-wired diamantés and ribbon.

Kliens
5 Noel Street
London W1F 8GD
020 7437 6162
www.kliens.co.uk
A huge array of haberdashery, including ribbons. Mail order available.

MacCulloch & Wallis
25–26 Dering Street
London W1S 1AT
020 7629 0311
www.macculloch-wallis.co.uk
Wide range of ribbons, plus bridal accessories and other haberdashery items. Mail order available.

V V Rouleaux
54 Sloane Square, Cliveden Place
London SW1W 8AX
020 7730 3125
www.vvrouleaux.com
Sophisticated ribbons and trims to suit any colour scheme.

Decorative bags

Accessorize
020 7313 3000
www.accessorize.co.uk
Branches nationwide.

Liberty
Regent Street
London W1B 5AH
020 7734 1234
www.liberty.co.uk

Floristry supplies
These companies stock a huge range including foam, tape, glue guns, wires, ribbon, corsage clips and magnets, bouquet holders, floristry scissors, pearl-headed pins and ready-to-decorate hair accessories, online and by mail order.

www.silkflowersdecoflora.co.uk
01900 872046

www.theessentialscompany.co.uk
01473 737567

www.rainbowfloristsupplies.co.uk
0800 212869

Index